THE WESSON OIL
COOKBOOK

SMITHMARK

INTRODUCTION

The Wesson name has been synonymous with great cooking since people first began cooking with vegetable oil. This book is a compilation of some of Wesson's most treasured recipes for cooking with Wesson Oil. If you have an appetite for good cooking, you will certainly enjoy this book. The recipes that follow will provide a wide variety of mouth-watering dishes that are certain to please you and your entire family at every meal.

Oils have been used for generations as a cooking agent as well as a flavor enhancer. Long before liquid oils became a staple in households around the world, the bulk of cooking was done with animal fat. It wasn't until certain technological developments occurred that the world saw the introduction of the first liquid vegetable oil. It revolutionized cooking around the world. Not only were liquid vegetable oils more versatile and longer lasting than their predecessors, but they contained no cholesterol and were lower in saturated fat.

Wesson played an integral role in the development of liquid cooking oils. David Wesson, a renowned chemist, introduced a process that led to the first vegetable oil on the market under the brand name "Wesson". His process created a pure, delicate oil with a light taste that was perfect for salads, cooking and baking. Today, Hunt-Wesson offers a full line of products to satisfy *every* cooking, frying and baking need.

Eating has always been one of America's favorite pastimes. Cooking with Wesson Oil promises to make that experience even better. Whether frying chicken, sautéing vegetables, or simply making a salad dressing, Hunt-Wesson has a product for all of your good cooking. Today the Wesson family of products has grown to include vegetable, corn, sunflower, canola and olive oils as well as cooking spray and shortening.

Our heritage and cooking tradition have a long successful history with the American family. It is our hope that Wesson products will continue to have a place in your family for generations to come. It is with great pleasure and pride that we share with you a sampling of the many wonderful recipes you can make even better when cooking with Wesson Oil.

CLB 2596
©1992 Colour Library Books Ltd, Godalming, Surrey, England.
© Recipes Hunt-Wesson Inc.
All rights reserved.
This edition published 1992 by
SMITHMARK Publishers Inc., 112 Madison Avenue, New York, NY 10016.
Printed and bound in singapore.
ISBN 0 8317 3191 5

SMITHMARK books are available for bulk sales promotion and premium use. For details write or telephone the Manager of Special Sales, SMITHMARK Publishers Inc., 112 Madison Avenue, New York, NY 10016. (212) 532-6600.

WESSON OIL IS A REGISTERED TRADEMARK OF HUNT-WESSON INC.

BLENDER POTATO SOUP

Makes 8 cups

This richly flavored soup gets its thickness from puréed vegetables rather than heavy creams.

½ cup Wesson Vegetable Oil
3 cups chopped celery
1½ cups chopped onions
½ tsp minced garlic
1 quart chicken broth
3 cups peeled, diced potatoes
¼ cup chopped fresh parsley
½ tsp salt
¼ tsp pepper
Shredded cheddar cheese

STEP 2

bring to a boil, reduce heat, and simmer, covered, 20 minutes or until potatoes are tender.

3. Pour *half* of mixture in blender and purée until smooth. Remove to second saucepan. Repeat with *remaining* mixture and add second puréed batch to first batch.

4. Ladle into warm bowls and sprinkle with cheese before serving.

STEP 1

1. In large saucepan, heat oil and sauté celery, onions and garlic until tender.

2. Stir in *remaining* ingredients *except* cheese;

STEP 3

Cook's Notes

⏱ TIME: Preparation takes about 30 minutes. Cooking takes 20 minutes.

✳ FREEZING: Soup may be covered tightly and frozen up to 2 months.

❓ VARIATIONS: Other favorite vegetables, such as broccoli, cauliflower or carrots may be substituted for celery.

FRIED MOZZARELLA STICKS

Makes 32 appetizers

This tasty recipe combines a golden crunchy coating with a smooth mild cheese interior to make a delightful appetizer your guests will rave over.

---

1 (16oz) bottle Wesson Vegetable Oil
1lb mozzarella cheese, cut into 32 sticks
½ cup all-purpose flour
2 eggs
2 Tbsps water
1¼ cups plain dry bread crumbs
½ tsp seasoned salt
¼ tsp garlic powder
Favorite dipping sauce

1. In medium heavy-bottom saucepan or electric skillet, heat oil to 370°F.

2. In bag, shake cheese with flour until well coated. In shallow bowl, beat eggs with water.

3. In second shallow bowl, combine bread crumbs, seasoned salt and garlic powder. Dip coated cheese sticks, one at a time, in egg mixture, then roll in crumb mixture until well coated.

4. Place cheese sticks on large baking sheet and chill one hour.

5. Fry sticks 3 or 4 at a time in hot oil about 3 to 5 seconds or until golden brown. Remove with slotted spoon and drain on paper towels. Serve with favorite dipping sauce such as Marinara Sauce.

STEP 3

STEP 5

Cook's Notes

🕐 TIME: Preparation takes about 20 minutes, chill 1 hour and frying takes about 30 minutes.

❓ VARIATION: Other types of cheese, such as Monterey Jack, hot pepper or herb-flavored cheeses may be substituted for mozzarella. Cheese may be coated and left to chill overnight for frying the next day.

HOT CHICKEN BITES
Makes about 4 dozen appetizers

These southwestern flavored chicken nuggets won't last long at your next party.

Chicken and Marinade

1½lbs boneless, skinless chicken breasts, cut in 2-inch cubes
Wesson Vegetable Oil
3 Tbsps Gebhardt Louisiana-Style Hot Sauce
1 Tbsp *each:* minced cilantro and lemon juice
¾ tsp *each:* garlic powder and ground cumin
½ tsp *each:* chili powder, salt and sugar
All-purpose flour
3 egg whites, beaten
Favorite dipping sauce

Breading

1¼ cups dried bread crumbs
1 tsp chili powder
½ tsp ground cumin
¼ tsp salt

1. In large bowl, combine chicken with ¼ cup oil, hot sauce, cilantro, lemon juice, garlic powder, cumin, chili powder, salt and sugar. Cover and refrigerate 6 hours or overnight.

2. In large heavy-bottom saucepan, heat 2 inches of oil to 325°F.

3. In small bowl, combine *breading* ingredients. Drain marinade from chicken and discard.

4. Lightly coat chicken cubes with flour, dip in egg whites, then coat completely with breading mixture.

5. Fry immediately in hot oil. Cook about 3 minutes or until golden brown and chicken is cooked through. Drain on paper towels. Serve hot with favorite dipping sauce.

STEP 2

STEP 4

Cook's Notes

⏱ TIME: Preparation takes about 30 minutes. Marinating takes 6 hours or overnight and frying takes about 30 minutes.

❓ VARIATIONS: Favorite dipping sauces may be salsa, ketchup or chili sauce. You may use your favorite hot sauce in place of the Gebhardt Louisiana-Style Hot Sauce. Marinated chicken may be left unbreaded, skewered on shisk kebabs with vegetables and grilled or broiled until chicken is cooked through.

SESAME RAMEN CHICKEN SALAD

Makes 9 cups salad

Ramen noodles go from soup to salad in this yummy Oriental salad that can go from church suppers to summer barbecues.

2 (3oz) pkgs. Chicken Flavor Ramen Noodles, broken and cooked according to package directions, drained and cooled
6 cups shredded green cabbage
3 cups diced cooked chicken
1 cup thinly sliced celery
1 cup sliced green onions
½ cup shredded carrots
½ cup Wesson Vegetable Oil
⅓ cup rice vinegar
3 Tbsps sugar
2 Tbsps toasted sesame seeds
1 Tbsp LaChoy Soy Sauce
1½ tsps salt
¾ tsp pepper
½ tsp minced fresh garlic

STEP 2

STEP 3

1. In large bowl, toss together ramen noodles, cabbage, chicken, celery, onions and carrots.

2. In small bowl, whisk together remaining ingredients until sugar dissolves.

3. Pour dressing over cabbage mixture and toss until all ingredients are well coated. Chill 1 hour before serving. Refrigerate if not being served immediately.

STEP 1

Cook's Notes

⏱ TIME: Preparation takes 20 minutes. Chilling takes 1 hour.

❓ VARIATION: Diced cooked turkey may be substituted for chicken.

INDIAN SUMMER STIR-FRY

Serves 4 to 6

What could be tastier or better for you than a fresh sautéed vegetable side dish seasoned with herbs and garlic!

3 Tbsps Wesson Vegetable Oil
3 medium carrots, thinly sliced
1 medium onion, sliced
1 small green bell pepper, cored and cubed
2 medium stalks celery, sliced
2 medium zucchini, sliced ¼-inch thick
1 cup fresh or frozen whole kernel corn
4 large mushrooms, sliced
1 tsp *each:* basil and garlic salt
¼ tsp pepper

1. In large skillet, heat oil and sauté carrots, onion, bell pepper, celery and zucchini until vegetables are lightly coated with oil.

2. Reduce heat to medium cover and cook 3 minutes, stirring once.

3. Add *remaining* ingredients and sauté 3 to 5 minutes or until mushrooms are tender. Do not overcook. Serve immediately.

STEP 1

Preparing vegetables

STEP 3

Cook's Notes

⏲ TIME: Preparation takes about 20 minutes. Cooking takes about 10 minutes.

❓ VARIATION: Vegetables may be cut up to a day ahead of time to be prepared at the cook's convenience.

MARINATED MUSHROOM ARTICHOKE SALAD

Makes 7 cups salad

This tasty salad travels well to picnics, tail-gate parties and church potlucks.

½ cup sliced green onions
⅓ cup Wesson Vegetable Oil
3 Tbsps white vinegar
2 Tbsps lemon juice
1 Tbsp Dijon mustard
1½ tsps basil
¾ tsp *each:* salt and pepper
½ tsp *each:* minced fresh garlic and sugar
6 cups thickly sliced mushrooms
1¼ cups red bell pepper cubes
1 (6oz) jar marinated artichoke hearts, undrained
Lettuce leaves

1. In large bowl, whisk together *first 10* ingredients.

2. Stir in *remaining* ingredients *except* lettuce. Marinate at least 2 hours or overnight.

3. Serve salad on lettuce leaves.

STEP 1

STEP 2

Cook's Notes

⌚ TIME: Preparation takes 15 to 20 minutes. Marinating takes 2 hours or overnight.

? VARIATION: Other colors of bell pepper may be used to substitute for red bell peppers.

ITALIAN TORTELLINI SALAD

Makes 7 cups salad

Make the night before and chill for a delicious picnic salad.

¼ cup Wesson Vegetable Oil
3 Tbsps cider vinegar
1 (0.7oz) pkg. dry Italian salad dressing mix
1 tsp basil
5 cups cooked cheese-filled tortellini
1 (15oz) can Hunt's Kidney Beans, well drained
1 (8oz) jar marinated artichoke hearts, undrained
1 cup thinly sliced celery
½ cup diced green bell pepper
1 (2.2oz) can sliced ripe black olives, drained
¼ cup chopped green onion

STEP 1

1. In large bowl, whisk together oil, vinegar, Italian dressing mix and basil.

2. Add remaining ingredients and toss until all ingredients are well coated.

3. Cover and chill 2 hours or overnight.

STEP 2

Cook's Notes

TIME: Preparation takes about 30 minutes plus at least 2 hours chilling time.

VARIATION: Chopped pepperoni or cooked ham may be added to salad.

COOK'S TIP: 1 (8oz) pkg. dry cheese-filled tortellini or 2 (9oz) pkgs. fresh cheese-filled tortellini, prepared according to package directions, makes 5 cups cooked cheese-filled tortellini.

BASIC MAYONNAISE

Makes 1 cup dressing

After you taste freshly made mayonnaise, you'll never want to go back to the supermarket variety.

1 large egg
½ tsp salt
¼ tsp dry mustard
¼ tsp white pepper
1 cup Wesson Vegetable Oil
1 Tbsp lemon juice

1. In blender container, place egg, salt, mustard and pepper. Cover and blend at medium-high speed 10 seconds.

2. With blender running, begin adding oil through opening in blender cover in a very thin stream.

3. When about ¼ cup oil remains and mayonnaise is thick, blend in lemon juice. Add remaining oil, with blender running, in a thin stream. Blend mayonnaise until very thick, stopping occasionally to stir in any unincorporated oil if necessary. Refrigerate until ready to use.

STEP 1

STEP 2

Cook's Notes

⌚ TIME: Preparation takes about 5 minutes. Blending takes about 15 minutes.

❓ VARIATION: Favorite dried or fresh herbs or spices may be added during blending.

ITALIAN DRESSING

Makes ¾ cup

A piquant vinaigrette with the right balance of herbs to enhance your salad.

½ cup Wesson Vegetable Oil
¼ cup cider vinegar
1 large clove garlic, minced
1 Tbsp minced green onion
1 Tbsp minced red bell pepper or pimiento
1½ tsps sugar
¾ tsp salt
⅛ tsp *each:* basil, pepper, oregano and thyme

1. In a jar with a tight-fitting lid, place all ingredients. Shake until well mixed.

STEP 2

STEP 1

STEP 3

2. Let stand 1 hour before serving to allow herbs to soften and flavors to blend.

3. Serve with your favorite vegetable salad. Refrigerate unused dressing.

Cook's Notes

⏱ TIME: Preparation takes about 10 minutes. Standing time takes 1 hour.

❓ VARIATION: Dressing may be used as a meat marinade and basting sauce.

CHEESY OVEN FRIES
Serves 8

These delicious crispy oven fries certainly won't be around as leftovers.

3 large russet potatoes, thinly sliced
2 cups thinly sliced onions
¼ cup Wesson Vegetable Oil
1½ tsps seasoned salt
¼ tsp *each:* garlic powder and pepper
1½ Tbsps grated Parmesan cheese

1. Preheat oven to 425°F.

2. In large bowl, toss potatoes and onions with oil until well coated. In cup, combine seasoned salt, garlic powder and pepper.

STEP 3

STEP 4

STEP 2

3. On large baking sheet, evenly spread potato mixture and sprinkle with spice mixture.

4. Bake for 15 minutes. Turn with spatula to redistribute, sprinkle with Parmesan and bake an additional 15 minutes.

Cook's Notes

 TIME: Preparation takes about 15 minutes. Baking takes 30 minutes.

? VARIATIONS: Other favorite spices may be added to spice mixture, such as chili powder, cumin or favorite herbs. Crumbled, cooked bacon may be stirred into potato mixture during last 15 minutes of baking.

HUSH PUPPIES

Makes 24

A crunchy southern fried delight that makes a nice change from biscuits or corn muffins.

3 cups Wesson Vegetable Oil
¾ cup *each:* all-purpose flour and cornmeal
2 tsps baking powder
1½ tsps sugar
¾ tsp garlic salt
½ cup *each:* minced fresh onion and milk
1 egg, beaten
1 green onion, minced

1. In deep heavy-bottom saucepan, heat oil to 375°F.

2. In large bowl, combine flour, cornmeal, baking powder, sugar and garlic salt.

3. In small bowl, beat together *remaining* ingredients. Stir milk mixture into flour mixture just until all ingredients are moistened; let stand 5 minutes.

4. Drop by teaspoonful into hot oil. Fry 3 to 4 minutes, until golden brown, turning as needed. Drain on paper towels.

STEP 3

STEP 4

Cook's Notes

TIME: Preparation takes about 20 minutes. Frying takes about 15 minutes.

SERVING IDEA: Perfect served with soup for a hearty lunch.

SHRIMP FRIED RICE

Makes 6 cups

This quick easy dish takes minutes to prepare and makes great use of leftover rice.

¼ cup Wesson Vegetable Oil
¾ cup *each:* diced celery and onion
1 tsp *each:* minced fresh garlic and gingerroot
2 eggs, beaten
4 cups cooked white rice
½lb small cooked, peeled shrimp
1 cup frozen peas and carrots, thawed
3 Tbsps LaChoy Soy Sauce
¼ tsp pepper

STEP 2

1. In large skillet, heat oil and sauté celery, onion, garlic and ginger until celery is tender.

2. Add eggs and cook, stirring constantly, until softy scrambled.

3. Stir in remaining ingredients and toss until mixture is well mixed and heated through.

STEP 3

Cook's Notes

⎣ TIME: Preparation takes about 10 minutes. Cooking takes about 15 minutes.

? VARIATIONS: Other frozen vegetables may be substituted for peas and carrots and 1 ½ cups chopped, cooked chicken or turkey may be substituted for shrimp.

SHRIMP TEMPURA

Serves 4

These are terrific for an interesting party entrée or try the batter on small shrimp for appetizers.

Wesson Vegetable Oil for frying
1lb large raw shrimp, cleaned and butterflied
1 cup ice water
1 cup all-purpose flour
1 egg yolk
2 Tbsps Wesson Vegetable Oil
1 tsp sugar
½ tsp *each:* salt and baking powder

1. Heat a large deep skillet, filled to ⅓ depth in oil, to 350°F. Check temperature with a deep-fat frying thermometer.

2. Wash shrimp; pat dry.

STEP 3

STEP 4

STEP 1

3. In a large bowl, whisk ice water and *next 6* ingredients until smooth.

4. Dip shrimp, a few at a time, in batter, letting excess drain off. Fry 2 to 3 minutes until light golden brown. Drain on paper towels and keep warm until ready to serve.

Cook's Notes

TIME: Preparation takes about 15 minutes. Frying takes about 15 minutes.

VARIATION: Favorite bite-size pieces of blanched vegetables may be used instead of shrimp. Shrimp may be served with favorite dipping sauce. If batter is not used immediately, keep covered in refrigerator. Whisk before using.

PAN-FRIED FISH

Serves 4 to 6

This light, golden, crunchy crust complements any favorite fish fillet.

¾ cup Wesson Vegetable Oil
1½lbs firm-fleshed white fish fillets
⅓ cup all-purpose flour
¼ cup cornmeal
1 tsp seasoned salt
⅛ tsp *each:* pepper and garlic powder
1 egg
2 Tbsps water

---

1. In large, heavy-bottom skillet, heat oil to 375°F.

2. Rinse fish and pat dry; set aside.

3. In large shallow bowl, combine flour, cornmeal, seasoned salt, pepper and garlic powder. In small shallow bowl, beat egg with water until well blended.

4. Dip fillets in egg mixture then coat with flour mixture making sure fish is completely coated.

5. Fry 2 to 3 minutes on each side or until fish flakes easily with a fork and crust is golden brown. Drain on paper towels.

STEP 4

STEP 1

STEP 5

Cook's Notes

TIME: Preparation takes about 10 minutes. Frying takes about 10 to 15 minutes.

? VARIATIONS: Flounder, Orange Roughy, Cod, Perch, Sole or Red Snapper may be used. Chicken breast fillets that have been pounded to ¼-inch thickness may be substituted for fish.

SATISFYIN' FRIED CHICKEN

Serves 4 to 6

Wesson's specialty of the house is golden brown and crunchy on the outside, tender and juicy on the inside.

1 cup Wesson Vegetable Oil
2½-3lbs frying chicken pieces
¾ cup all-purpose flour
1½ tsps salt
1 tsp *each:* pepper and paprika
½ tsp *each:* onion powder and rubbed sage
¼ tsp garlic powder
1 egg
2 Tbsps water

1. In heavy-bottom skillet, heat 1 cup Wesson Oil to 375°F. Rinse chicken and pat dry.

2. In bag, combine flour, salt, pepper, paprika, onion powder, sage and garlic powder.

3. In shallow bowl, beat egg with water.

4. Shake chicken, one piece at a time, in flour mixture until coated. Dip in egg, then shake again in flour mixture until completely coated.

5. Fry chicken, skin side down, for 12 minutes. Turn and fry, covered, 10 minutes.

6. Uncover and fry an additional 3 to 5 minutes until chicken is tender and juices run clear.

STEP 1

STEP 5

Cook's Notes

TIME: Preparation takes about 15 minutes. Frying takes 25 to 30 minutes.

SERVING IDEA: Serve hot for Sunday dinner or take along on a picnic.

CURRIED PORK CHOPS AND VEGETABLES

Serves 5

These spicy chops are colorful and mouthwatering. Serve with rice and a crisp green salad to round out the meal.

5 ½-inch thick loin pork chops
3 Tbsps all-purpose flour
1 tsp salt
3 Tbsps Wesson Vegetable Oil
1 medium onion, cut in eighths
1 medium green bell pepper, cored and cut in thin
    strips
1 medium zucchini, cut in julienne strips
2 tsps minced garlic
1 (8oz) can Hunt's Whole Tomatoes, undrained
    and crushed
1 (8oz) can Hunt's Tomato Sauce
1½ tsps curry powder
¼ tsp pepper
⅛ tsp cayenne pepper

STEP 2

STEP 4

1. In bag, shake chops with flour and salt.

2. In large skillet, in hot oil, brown chops in oil; remove and set aside.

3. In drippings, sauté onion, bell pepper, zucchini and garlic until vegetables are tender.

4. Stir in remaining ingredients; return chops to pan. Spoon sauce over chops; cover and simmer 10 to 15 minutes or until chops are cooked through.

Cook's Notes

⌞ TIME: Preparation takes about 15 minutes. Cooking takes about 30 minutes total time.

❓ VARIATION: Boneless, skinless chicken breasts may be substituted for pork chops.

CHICKEN CACCIATORE

Serves 4 to 6

To make your meal complete, just add a salad and a loaf of crusty bread to soak up the rich sauce.

1 (3 to 4lb) cut-up chicken
Salt and pepper
All-purpose flour
¼ cup Wesson Vegetable Oil
½lb sliced mushrooms
1½ cups sliced onions
1 tsp minced garlic
1 (14½oz) can Hunt's Stewed Tomatoes
1 (8oz) can Hunt's Tomato Sauce
½ tsp *each:* basil, oregano and thyme
¼ cup dry white wine

3. In drippings, sauté mushrooms, onions and garlic until tender.

4. Add chicken and *remaining* ingredients except

STEP 3

STEP 2

STEP 4

1. Season chicken with salt and pepper and coat lightly with flour.

2. In Dutch oven, brown chicken in oil; remove and set aside.

wine. Coat chicken with sauce and simmer, covered, 30 minutes.

5. Add wine, cover and simmer an additional 15 minutes.

Cook's Notes

⏳ TIME: Preparation takes about 15 to 20 minutes. Total cooking takes 45 minutes.

❓ VARIATIONS: Boneless chicken parts may be substituted for a cut-up chicken. Recipe may be made the day before serving. Cover and refrigerate overnight, then reheat the next day.

FLANK STEAK TERIYAKI

Serves 6 to 8

Serve with rice or buttered noodles and a colorful vegetable side dish for a quick and delicious meal.

½ cup LaChoy Soy Sauce
⅓ cup Wesson Vegetable Oil
¼ cup honey
2 Tbsps red wine vinegar
1 clove garlic, minced
1 tsp minced gingerroot
1½ to 2lbs flank steak

---

1. In glass or plastic rectangular dish, stir together all ingredients except steak.

2. Score steak on both sides; place in marinade.

Cover and refrigerate 2 hours, turning once.

3. Broil steak 6 inches from heat source, about 5 minutes on each side or to desired doneness.

4. To serve, cut in thin slices across the grain.

STEP 2

STEP 1

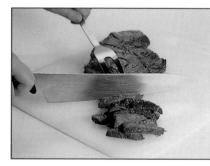

STEP 3

Cook's Notes

🕐 TIME: Preparation takes about 10 minutes, marinating 2 hours and broiling or grilling takes 10 minutes.

❓ VARIATIONS: After slicing, beef may be cut in smaller pieces and added to a green salad for lunch or a light supper. Before broiling, meat may be cut in slices, then stir-fried with favorite vegetables.

SAVORY BEEF STEW

Makes 8 cups stew

A bowl of this hearty stew with cornbread or a crusty roll will warm up any cold winter night.

1½lbs lean stew beef, cut in bite-size pieces
¼ cup all-purpose flour
½ tsp seasoned salt
2 medium onions, cut in 1-inch chunks
⅓ cup Wesson Vegetable Oil
1 (14½oz) can beef broth
1 (8oz) can Hunt's Tomato Sauce
2 medium potatoes, peeled and cubed
3 stalks celery, cut in 1-inch chunks
2 medium carrots, cut in 1-inch chunks
¾ tsp salt
½ tsp pepper
¼ tsp *each:* marjoram and thyme

STEP 2

STEP 3

STEP 1

1. In bag, toss beef with flour and seasoned salt.

2. In Dutch oven, in hot oil, brown beef with onions until onions are tender.

3. Add remaining ingredients; stir until well mixed. Bring to a boil, reduce heat and simmer, covered, 90 minutes or until beef is tender.

Cook's Notes

 TIME: Preparation takes about 20 minutes. Cooking takes about 2 hours.

VARIATION: A 10oz box of frozen green beans, corn, lima beans or mixed vegetables may be added to the stew. Stew may be made the day before and reheated.

LEMON-BLUEBERRY MUFFINS

Makes 12 muffins

A light, fruity treat for breakfast or afternoon tea!

1¾ cups all-purpose flour
¾ cup sugar
2 tsps baking powder
½ tsp salt
¼ tsp ground cinnamon
1 cup milk
⅓ cup Wesson Vegetable Oil
2 Tbsps lemon juice
1 egg, beaten
1 tsp *each:* grated lemon peel and vanilla extract
1 cup fresh or frozen blueberries

1. Preheat oven to 375°F. Grease a 12-cup muffin pan.

2. In large bowl, combine flour, sugar, baking powder, salt and cinnamon.

3. In second bowl, mix together remaining ingredients except blueberries. Pour milk mixture into flour mixture and stir just until all ingredients are moistened. Gently fold in blueberries. Spoon batter into prepared muffin pan.

4. Bake for 20 to 25 minutes or until muffins test done with wooden pick.

STEP 3

STEP 2

STEP 4

Cook's Notes

⌚ TIME: Preparation takes about 15 minutes. Baking takes 20 to 25 minutes.

✳ FREEZING: Muffins may be wrapped well and kept frozen up to 1 month.

? VARIATION: Combine ⅓ cup powdered sugar with 2 tablespoons lemon juice until sugar dissolves. Spoon glaze over warm muffins before serving.

APPLE STREUSEL OATMEAL MUFFINS

Makes 12

An old-fashioned healthy treat filled with oats, apples, raisins and other goodies.

Streusel

¼ cup *each:* all-purpose flour and old-fashioned rolled oats
3 Tbsps chopped pecans
2 Tbsps Wesson Vegetable Oil
2 Tbsps packed light brown sugar
¼ tsp ground cinnamon

Muffins

1 cup all-purpose flour
¾ cup old-fashioned rolled oats
½ cup packed light brown sugar
1 Tbsp baking powder
1½ tsps ground cinnamon
½ tsp *each:* salt and ground nutmeg
¼ tsp ground cloves
¾ cup unsweetened applesauce
½ cup golden raisins
⅓ cup Wesson Vegetable Oil
1 egg, beaten

1. Preheat oven to 375°F. Grease a 12-cup muffin pan.

2. In small bowl, stir *streusel* ingredients together with a fork until well-blended and mixture is crumbly; set aside.

3. In large bowl, combine flour, oats, brown sugar, baking powder, cinnamon, salt, nutmeg and cloves.

4. In medium bowl, combine *remaining* ingredients. Stir applesauce mixture into flour mixture just until all ingredients are moistened.

5. Spoon batter evenly into prepared muffin cups. Sprinkle streusel topping over each muffin.

6. Bake for 30 minutes or until muffins test done with wooden pick.

STEP 4

STEP 5

Cook's Notes

TIME: Preparation takes about 10 minutes. Baking takes 30 minutes.

? VARIATION: Walnuts may be used instead of pecans.

UPSIDE DOWN BANANA PECAN MUFFINS

Makes 14

Like Sticky Buns and Banana Bread, only faster and just as delicious.

½ cup packed light brown sugar
⅓ cup butter, softened
⅔ cup chopped pecans
2 cups all-purpose flour
½ cup sugar
1 Tbsp baking powder
1 tsp ground cinnamon
½ tsp salt
2 eggs
½ cup Wesson Vegetable Oil
2 ripe bananas, mashed
1 tsp vanilla extract

1. Preheat oven to 375°F. Grease 14 muffin cups.

2. In small bowl, combine brown sugar, butter and pecans. Place *1 tablespoon* nut mixture into prepared muffin cups; set aside.

STEP 4

STEP 6

STEP 2

3. In medium bowl, combine flour, sugar, baking powder, cinnamon and salt.

4. In small bowl, beat together eggs, oil, bananas and vanilla. Stir oil mixture into flour mixture just until all ingredients are moistened. Fill prepared muffin cups with batter.

5. Bake for 20 minutes or until tests done with wooden pick. Serve warm.

6. To serve, invert muffins on plate.

Cook's Notes

⤵ TIME: Preparation takes 20 minutes. Baking takes 20 minutes.

○ SERVING IDEA: Great for breakfast, an afternoon snack or dessert.

？ VARIATIONS: Walnuts may be substituted for pecans.

CINNAMON STREUSEL COFFEE CAKE

Makes one 8-inch coffee cake

This spicy cinnamon coffee cake will bring the family running to the table.

1½ cups all-purpose flour
½ cup *each:* packed light brown sugar and
    chopped nuts
⅓ cup sugar
1 tsp ground cinnamon
½ tsp ground nutmeg
½ cup Wesson Vegetable Oil
½ cup buttermilk
2 tsps baking powder
1 egg, beaten
½ tsp *each:* baking soda and salt

1. Preheat oven to 350°F. Grease an 8-inch baking pan.

2. In large bowl, combine flour, brown sugar, nuts, sugar, cinnamon and nutmeg. With a fork, stir in oil until mixture is crumbly. Remove ½ *cup* streusel mixture; set aside.

3. Add *remaining* ingredients to bowl and stir until well blended. Pour into prepared pan; sprinkle with reserved streusel mixture.

4. Bake for 35 minutes or until cake tests done with wooden pick.

STEP 3

STEP 2

STEP 4

Cook's Notes

⌚ TIME: Preparation takes about 15 minutes. Baking takes 35 minutes.

❓ VARIATIONS: Sour cream or plain yogurt may be substituted for buttermilk. For a ready-to-bake cake for breakfast, make cake but do not bake. Cover, refrigerate, then bake in the morning. Baking time will be slightly longer.

WESSON'S HUMMINGBIRD CAKE

Makes one 10-inch tube cake

A traditional southern cake, rich with fruit and nuts, that keeps well and can be served warm or cooled.

Cake

3 cups all-purpose flour
1½ tsps *each:* baking soda and ground cinnamon
¾ tsp salt
1½ cups sugar
4 medium bananas, mashed (about 1½ cups)
1 cup Wesson Vegetable Oil
1 cup *each:* finely chopped pecans and flaked coconut
1 (8oz) can crushed pineapple
3 eggs
1 tsp vanilla extract

Glaze

⅓ cup powdered sugar
2 tsps lemon juice

STEP 3

STEP 6

STEP 1

1. Preheat oven to 350°F. Grease and flour a 10-inch tube pan.

2. In large bowl, combine flour, baking soda, cinnamon and salt.

3. In second bowl, beat together remaining cake ingredients until well blended. Fold oil mixture into flour mixture just until all ingredients are moistened. Spoon batter into prepared pan.

4. Bake for 1 hour or until cake tests done with wooden pick. Cool in pan 30 minutes.

5. Meanwhile, in small bowl, mix together glaze ingredients until sugar completely dissolves.

6. Place cake on plate and drizzle glaze evenly over warm cake.

Cook's Notes

⌙ TIME: Preparation takes about 15 minutes. Baking takes 1 hour.

? VARIATION: Cake may be dusted with powdered sugar for a festive look.

✳ FREEZING: Wrap cake well and keep frozen for up to 4 months.

HARVEST APPLE CAKE

Makes one 9-inch layer cake

Celebrate the return of fall with this tasty treat of spicy apple cake topped with luscious cream cheese frosting!

Cake
2½ cups all-purpose flour
1 tsp *each:* baking soda and cinnamon
½ tsp *each:* nutmeg and salt
¼ tsp ground cloves
2 cups sugar
1 cup Wesson Vegetable Oil
3 eggs
3 cups peeled, cored and grated apples
1 cup chopped walnuts
1 tsp vanilla extract

Frosting
1lb powdered sugar
1 (8oz) pkg. cream cheese, softened
¼ cup butter, softened
1 Tbsp apple juice or milk
½ tsp vanilla extract

STEP 4

STEP 5

1. Preheat oven to 350°F. Grease and flour two 9-inch round baking pans.

2. In small bowl, combine flour, soda, cinnamon, nutmeg, salt and cloves.

3. In large bowl, beat together sugar, oil and eggs until well blended. Stir in apples, walnuts and vanilla.

4. Beat flour mixture into apple mixture just until all ingredients are well mixed. Pour batter into prepared pans.

5. Bake for 35 minutes or until cake tests done with wooden pick. Cool completely on cake racks.

6. In large bowl, combine all frosting ingredients. Beat with an electric mixer until smooth.

7. Ice cooled cake with frosting.

Cook's Notes

TIME: Preparation takes about 30 minutes. Baking takes 35 minutes. Cooling and frosting takes about 1 hour.

VARIATION: Other favorite nuts, such as pecans may be substituted for walnuts. Chopped walnuts may be sprinkled on top of frosted cake for a festive touch.

FAMOUS WESSON OIL BROWNIES

Makes 16 brownies

You can't beat these quick homemade treats for lunch boxes or as a goody for after school.

2 eggs
1 cup sugar
⅓ cup Wesson Oil
2oz unsweetened chocolate, melted and cooled
1 tsp vanilla extract
¾ cup all-purpose flour
¾ tsp salt
½ tsp baking powder
¾ cup chopped nuts

STEP 3

and vanilla.

3. Add flour, salt and baking powder; mix well. Stir in nuts. Spoon into prepared dish.

4. Bake for 35 minutes. Cut into squares when cooled.

STEP 2

1. Preheat oven to 325°F. Grease an 8-inch square glass baking dish.

2. In large mixer bowl, at medium speed, beat egg and sugar 2 minutes. Beat in oil, melted chocolate

STEP 4

Cook's Notes

🕒 TIME: Preparation takes about 10 minutes. Baking takes 35 minutes.

❓ VARIATION: Brownies may be frosted, if desired. Coconut may be substituted for nuts.

COCOA SNACK CAKE

Makes 16 servings

Great for lunch boxes, after school treats and picnics.

1½ cups all-purpose flour
1 cup sugar
¼ cup unsweetened cocoa powder
1 tsp baking soda
¾ tsp salt
¼ tsp ground cinnamon
½ cup Wesson Vegetable Oil
½ cup *each:* buttermilk and water
1 egg
1 tsp vanilla extract
½ cup *each:* semi-sweet chocolate chips and
    chopped nuts
Powdered sugar

1. Preheat oven to 325°F. Grease and flour an 8-inch square baking pan.

2. In large mixing bowl, stir together first 6 ingredients.

3. Add oil, buttermilk, water, egg and vanilla and beat with an electric mixer on low speed just until all ingredients are blended. Beat one minute longer until batter is smooth.

4. Stir in chocolate chips and nuts. Pour into prepared pan.

5. Bake for 50 minutes or until cake tests done with wooden pick. Cool in pan. Dust with powdered sugar. Cut into sixteen 2-inch squares.

STEP 3

STEP 4

STEP 5

Cook's Notes

TIME: Preparation takes about 15 minutes. Baking takes 50 minutes.

? VARIATIONS: Cake may be frosted with favorite icing instead of powdered sugar.

MOLASSES SUGAR COOKIES

Makes about 4 dozen cookies

These crisp spicy cookies taste as terrific as they look.

1⅔ cups sugar
1½ cups Wesson Vegetable Oil
½ cup light molasses
2 eggs
4 cups all-purpose flour
4 tsps baking soda
2 tsps ground cinnamon
1 tsp salt
Sugar

---

1. Preheat oven to 375°F.

2. In large bowl, combine 1⅔ cups sugar, oil, molasses and eggs; beat well.

3. Sift flour, baking soda, cinnamon and salt into oil mixture; mix well. Cover and refrigerate dough at least 30 minutes.

4. Form into 1-inch balls, roll in sugar. Place 2 inches apart on ungreased baking sheets.

5. Bake for 10 to 12 minutes or until golden brown. Let cookies cool slightly before removing from pans. Cool on racks. Store cookies in an airtight container.

STEP 4

STEP 3

STEP 4

Cook's Notes

🕐 TIME: Preparation takes about 15 minutes. Chilling takes 30 minutes and baking takes about 45 minutes (all batches).

❓ VARIATIONS: Dough may be left to chill overnight. To make ginger cookies, add 1 teaspoon ground ginger.

CHEESE BISCUITS

Makes about 5 dozen

These tasty party snacks are easy to prepare and can be made in advance.

2 cups shredded sharp cheddar cheese
1⅓ cups all-purpose flour
1 tsp salt
½ tsp garlic powder
¼ tsp dill weed
⅛ tsp cayenne pepper
⅓ cup Wesson Vegetable Oil
¼ cup milk

STEP 1

1. In medium bowl, combine cheese, flour, salt, garlic powder, dill weed and cayenne pepper.

2. Add oil and milk; stir until mixture holds together when squeezed into a ball. Divide dough in half and shape each portion into a roll 1-inch in diameter. Wrap in plastic wrap and chill 2 hours or overnight.

3. Preheat oven to 375°F.

4. Slice biscuits about ¼-inch thick. Place slices on ungreased baking sheet without biscuits touching.

5. Bake for 10 to 12 minutes or until lightly browned. Store in an airtight container.

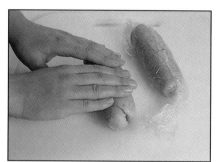

STEP 2

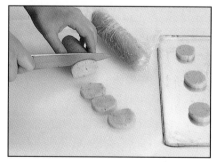

STEP 4

Cook's Notes

⏱ TIME: Preparation takes about 25 minutes. Baking takes 10 to 12 minutes per batch.

❓ VARIATIONS: Before chilling, dough may be rolled out ⅛ to ¼-inch thick and cut in various shapes or cut in strips then twisted. Chill before baking as directed.

CORNBREAD

Serves 8 to 10

*Serve hot with butter and honey or round out a
meal with chili or soup and salad.*

1 cup yellow cornmeal
1 cup all-purpose flour
3 Tbsps sugar
1 Tbsp baking powder
¾ tsp salt
1 cup milk
⅓ cup Wesson Vegetable Oil
1 egg

1. Preheat oven to 400°F. Grease an 8-inch baking pan.

2. In large bowl, combine cornmeal, flour, sugar, baking powder and salt.

STEP 3

3. In second bowl, beat together milk, oil and egg. Stir milk mixture into flour mixture just until all ingredients are moistened; pour into prepared baking pan.

4. Bake for 25 minutes or until tests done with a wooden pick. Cool and cut into squares.

STEP 1

STEP 4

Cook's Notes

TIME: Preparation takes about 15 minutes. Baking takes 25 minutes.

VARIATION: Batter may be baked in greased muffin tins. Bake 15 to 20 minutes. Makes 12 muffins.

INDEX

Photographed by Peter Barry
Recipes prepared and styled by Helen Burdett
Project co-ordination by Hanni Penrose
Edited by Jillian Stewart
Designed by Sally Strugnell